ISBN 978-1-331-31945-0
PIBN 10173757

Vindication.

THE restless citizens of a Republic too often " lash the ocean to waft a feather." But the late address of the Secretary of State is an object of no trifling magnitude : and though from some quarters the fiercest fury of wind and wave has beaten upon it, we trust, that its principles are " founded on a rock," and will prove imperishable.

The author himself, too, one of our ripest scholars, an experienced statesman, and the citizen of sterling private worth, on whom the eyes of America are turned as the candidate for her highest honours : this man must expect to become a frequent mark for the shafts of envy and faction. Far be it from us to pretend, that either he or his oration are invulnerable. But we do aver, whether these strictures be found in the dull orgies of *Relfe's Gazette*, and the Cassius croakings of the *Richmond Enquirer*, or in oracular reviews from the "Emporium of Literature," that their manner is generally injudicious and the matter of some of them most derogatory to the true interests of our country. Of candid and temperate criticism we surely feel no disposition to complain, Its influence is salutary. But why is not the graceless task of covering with sneers, sarcasm and coarse calumny our own literature and government, left to the professional libellers of England? Admit that the address of Mr. Adams is not altogether a fault-less production ; yet why should this circumstance be reiterated as an heinous offence, when every thing human is obnoxious to a similar charge?

The address is not a folio volume, nor the revised copy of a dissertation after the corrections of twenty years ; but it is the fugitive and almost extemporaneous effusion of the moment. Is the genuine test of its merits, then, the feebleness of a period, the misuse of an expletive, the transposition of an adverb? Let us rather ask, whatever may be its imperfections, who is there among the disciples of that republicanism, which broke our colonial chains, that has not felt his heart burn at the perusal of it? And if this hath been its operation, if it hath kindled in us a more ardent glow of patriotism, and roused that fearlessness and proud scorn of British oppression, which redeemed our fathers, what more ought we to expect? Would to God, that, on our national anniversary, we might oftener meet with productions breathing like this an inspiring energy from the consecrated principles of our revolution. The history of free States is full of warning upon their degeneracy : but it is not, that they are often betrayed or forcibly enslaved. On the contrary, they are prone to slumber over small encroachments—to forget the original and saving spirit of their institutions : and whether, in the end, they sink the victims of foreign domination, or dwindle into "hewers of wood" to some domestic usurper, their fall is in general irrecoverable and base. It is only when the noblest sons of a Republic are willing to sound the tocsin and recal her backsliding race to elementary principles ; when some Codrus offers to close the fatal breach, or some Cato dares to disturb their effeminate dreams, that hope "waves her golden hair" over fond perspectives of the future.

But so general an answer to the grave charges against the address may be construed into an implication of their truth. We shall, therefore, proceed to a more specific examination of them. They relate to the incorrectness of its political principles—its improper temper—faulty style—injustice to English literature, and inappropriate character, when viewed in connection with the rank of the author.

Every friend of our independence ought to have anticipated, that an address in its praise would incur the censure of critics, who, in making the censure, are forced to admit, that they " seem to write a defence of England and of English politics." Can it be doubted, that such a defence was attempted, when they stigmatize the address as mere " stuff," vilify its principles as stale, and deny to the declaration which Mr. Adams read any excellence of sentiment not pirated by our fathers from the institutions of England? But, if the institutions of England rest on the same theory with ours—why did Mercer and Montgomery bleed to establish independence? and why are we not now cursed with a King, a Peerage, a National Church and an omnipotent Parliament? On the contrary, if the fountain of power be here different—the delegation of it different—its checks different—its administration as different as the poles are distant; then why is the importance of the Declaration of Independence belittled ; and why are railing accusations brought against the address for its eulogy of the Declaration?

As an illustration of these remarks, Mr. Adams is distinctly charged with ignorance or falsehood ; because he avers that this immortal State Paper, was the " first solemn declaration of a nation of the only legitimate foundation of civil government."

To prove the insolent charge of ignorance or falsehood, the reviewer adds, that " the grand principle" in the Declaration was long before discovered. Does the address deny that ? It only says, that this principle was then for the first time *solemnly* declared by " *a nation.*" Not that there had been in former ages no Brutuses, nor Hampdens, nor Sidneys, nor Lockes.

Again the reviewer adds, that this principle had previously been applied in some instances in England and elsewhere. The address, so far from gainsaying this, only observes, that it had not before been solemnly declared by a *nation*, "as the only legitimate *foundation* of civil government." The very extracts, introduced by the reviewer from Burke, show, that the English nation, often as the agony of oppression has driven them into rebellion, have never considered this

principle as the " only legitimate foundation" of her government.

The merest tyro in her laws, too, cannot
be ignorant, that in both theory and practice
her people are not the fountain of either power or honour : that her Parliament is omnipotent, and, so far from being checked by the
judiciary or the elective franchise, can subject, and at times have subjected both to the
tenure of her will : that the Representative
principle applies only to a portion of Parliament, and even that portion is not elected on
any equal ratio of numbers or property :
that however elected, it is also subject to be
defeated in every measure by a Peerage,
who hold their seats in perfect contempt of
both the people and of any Representative principle : and that even this Peerage as well as
the House of Commons are powerless before
a King, who rests his throne on conquest and
inheritance.

It is false, too, that he has ever been dis-
placed by the People. Even Parliament
have never attempted to introduce a succes-
sion, not founded on legitimate descent from
Danish pirates or Norman robbers. Indeed
the principles of legitimacy are branded on
every page of her history, and her people

have scarce a charter or a right which has not been wrested by the sword. But it is the tenure by which her population hold their rights, which constitutes the great distinction and which elevates the humblest American to greatness and degrades the proudest Briton into a slave.

When goslin reviewers, therefore, sneer at "such stuff as this address is made of," they forget that Mr. Adams was not bred in the court of Sardanapalus, but in the primitive puritan shades of a young Republic; that to him who was rocked in the cradle of the revolution, both vice and slavery are monsters of "hideous mien," and that the courage as well as liberty to denounce them were his birth-right. Nor is it any reproach on such a man to be libelled in a place, where for twenty years the author of the Declaration of Independence was a standing theme of newspaper ribaldry, and where, during the same period, British reviewers, spies, clerks and stage actors have been welcomed to the domestic hearth with prodigal hospitality.

If, in this "era of good feelings," hopes have been indulged, that our own country, her statesmen and institutions would escape further obloquy, we feel regret, that whenever England happens to become the object of just rebuke, those hopes should fade. But we will not part with them altogether. A few noisy demagogues are not always the oracles of a large population. We trust there is still a redeeming spirit of republicanism and national feeling hovering near the mounds of Bunker's Hill.

Another specific and "great objection" to the address is said to be "the temper which it discovers towards England." This "temper," I suppose, consists principally in the truth and soberness of its account of the causes of our separation from her. If England and her kings in that account appear oppressive, Mr. Adams, forsooth, has discovered an ill "temper." With a few among us, England is, indeed, "the bulwark of our religion, and her monarch "the defender of the Faith." How, then, can their immoralities be exposed without sacrilege and the worst of "temper?" But Mr. Adams has "out-heroded Herod." On the very anniversary of our separation from England, when about to read the Declaration of Independence, which is filled with a catalogue of her aggressions and of her monarch's political sins, the orator himself has travelled out of the record and had the bad "temper" to allude to both of them. He has actually hinted at "frailties" in George III. when our fathers, in the public document then in his hand, only pronounced him "a prince, whose character is marked by every act which may define a tyrant." Though history, even English history, in the courage and integrity of truth, has "damned to everlasting fame" its own king John, as a tyrant—its own Henry IV. as an usurper—its Richard III. a murderer—its Henry VIII. a blue beard, and its Charles II. both infidel and voluptuary: yet an American, who owes neither allegiance nor veneration to any of the kingly tribe, must not presume to breathe aloud the slightest reflection upon that one of them, whose oppressions scourged our fathers into a revolution. Indeed it is often reiterated that Mr. Adams ought to have been totally silent concerning George III. What! when the orator read and commented on the Declaration of Independence—more than three fifths of which is devoted to a specific catalogue of wrongs expressly imputed to George III.—was it, in truth, his duty to make no allusion to him? Was his tongue to become palsied and mute ? or rather would he not have been justified in exhibiting the "temper" and in echoing the avowal of Jefferson and Franklin, that the history of that prince was " a history of repeated injuries and usurpations, all having in direct object the establishment of an absolute tyranny over these States ?"

We really fear, from the tone of our present unfledged race of politicians, that the Declaration of Independence is becoming a forgotten state paper ; and, in admiration of " the ruler of the waves," that the principles of that Declaration and the patriots of that age are about to be consigned to oblivion.

A part of the ill " temper" of Mr. Adams is also said to be evinced in the manner of his allusions. It wants sycophancy, and varnish, and Chesterfieldianism, and Castlereaghism : as if, in speaking of a man, publicly denounced by our sires for " a tyrant," one of their sons was bound to apologize for their simple honesty and to sweeten his own opinions with civet.

I must confess my own astonishment at the gentleness of Mr. Adams, imbued as his

mind is and ought to be with our revolutionary wrongs, and the spirit of our present institutions. The private character of George
III. and his personal calamities are one
thing. His official and political sins are another, and demand the deep execration of
Americans in every age. They were the
deeds of a public man. Their operation ex-
tended over two continents. Their example
is the public property of orators, as well as
of historians and statesmen. Future gene_
rations, who cannot escape their influence,
are to be reminded of their origin. And we
are yet to learn, that either good taste, deco-
rum, or national comity require such a "temper" in Americans as consists in sealing
their lips over the crimes, and in blazoning
only the virtues of those public men, who
have been their inveterate enemies.

It is foul misrepresentation to allege, also,
that Mr. Adams "undertakes to pronounce
on what in any particular case will be the
judgments at the bar of divine mercy." He
merely hazards a conjecture, that the personal sufferings of the last days of the British
King "may" have atoned for former political errors. What is there in this, which in-
dicates a "temper," presumptuous, irreve-

rent or harsh? The departed spirits of our fathers might justly rebuke us from the skies, if, on the day when their colonial chains were burst—chains imposed by England and rivetted to the bone by George III. we had become so degenerate as to blush at an allusion to the "frailties" of their "tyrant." And yet the loyal reviewer shudders at such "absolute rudeness," and perfumes his pages with incense to England, as the "greatest" "nation on earth."

The third charge against the address relates merely to its style of composition. One illustration is called "a school-boy figure;" another, "forced and unnatural;" and, indeed, a page or two is said to be written "in extremely bad taste." Yet none of these arrogant assertions are supported by reference to particular rules of criticism or grammar, which Mr. Adams has been so wicked as to violate. It would have been most unwise in the orator to have supposed, that on a great national jubilee, when every heart around him throbbed with exultation, he alone was bound to be dull, and dry, and frozen.

The charge of "obscurity" in the last sentence of the address has some plausibility. But this arises from the length of the sen-

tence and from inattention to what precedes
it. The reviewer is sadly puzzled to discov-
er who directs us to " go," and " like" whom
we are to act. Yet, to use his own *elegant*
language, " every one may guess *out* for himself," that it is the spirit, which dictated the
Declaration of Independence, that exhorts us
to " go" and to act "like" those, to whom the
Declaration was dictated. " Go," says that
spirit, and cherish their devotion to liberty—
their sleepless vigilance—their abhorrence of
British oppression—their integrity to their
own altars and homes.

The reviewer, in fine, has made the nota-
ble discovery, that the whole address is un-
distinguished " from the ordinary crowd of
performances on the same occasion." And
yet its importance is such as to elicit from
him twenty or thirty pages of criticism, and
some of its topics are " well selected," and
indeed " the general plan" of the whole oration, " very happy." He has made this no-
table discovery of its mediocrity, too, after
the address had been reprinted and read
and admired from Maine to Florida. We
can "guess *out*," likewise, that such sheer
impudence has seldom been found in a
puny pamphleteer as to preface this dis-

covery with a remark, that *he was invited to insert it in the North American;* but that his eagerness to pluck earlier laurels from the public prevented a compliance with the request. If that Journal, with the unfortunate Athenian fickleness of the people among whom it is printed, had changed, in three brief months, its grave censures on England, and her politicians into abuse of America, and had proceeded to reprobate the strictures before made as " dirty work," and avowed a readiness to perform penance for the "controversy," we must confess, that our mortification at such an apostacy would have been extreme. Not that Englishmen enough by birth and a few by principle have ever been wanting in our northern metropolis to become " the champions of Britannia," and " the chivalrous knights of chartered liberties and the rotten borough;" and to shout with the reviewer, that by England "the whole civilized world has been saved from the sternest despotism which ever oppressed it." As if to be saved from a single despot, for the purpose of wearing the chains of an " Holy Alliance" of despots, demanded as loud hosannas as the salvation by the Cross. But that native Americans—who have meditated on our history—studied the principles of our government—admired the virtues of our immediate fathers, and felt, in their own persons, " the scoffs which patient merit of the unworthy takes"—would become such miscreant wretches as to lick the hand which smites them, is not to be credited. With all intelligent politicians, the question is not whether England be more of a paradise than America for kings, nobles and priests ; but whether the great mass of her population participate in such rights and comforts—whether the form of her government and the condition of her morals be so pre-eminent as to justify the unsparing abuse, which her travellers, orators and authors constantly heap upon us.

Another accusation against Mr. Adams, is, that he decries "the rich and noble literature of England." But it is to be remembered, that every thing, which he utters on this point, is in answer to a taunting interrogatory in the Edinburgh Review as to what America has done " for the benefit of mankind :" and that his remarks are directed, not to her comparative progress in belles-lettres, but chiefly to what Americans have atchieved in those sciences and arts, which

confer direct usefulness on the great mass of
society. In his animated survey of this subject, if some retaliatory "sneers" escape
from him, the fraudulent reviewer knows, it
is not at the "rich and noble literature of
England;" but at the restless attempts of her
scholars to aggrandize abstruse and specula-
tive researches, in their " benefit to mankind," over the exertions, which distinguish
America for the amelioration of the lower
orders of society—for her improvements in
government, her inventions in mechanics.
If a sentence or two flames with retorted
" bitterness," it is not towards Bacon or
Locke ; but against the purblind politicians,
who can discern no " benefit to mankind" in
reducing to practice what others have only
suggested. If his "manner be reproachful,"
the reviewer knows it is not at " Miss Edge-
worth and the author of Waverley," but at
the myriads of "fustian romances," with
which England has deluged and enervated
the rising generation, and which are urged
by her as a " benefit to mankind" in competi-
tion with what has here been atchieved in the
education and comforts of the poor—in the
rights of conscience—the security of property—and the universal enjoyment of equal lib-

erty. Not at the *moral* verse of Shakspeare, Milton and Cowper, but at the " spawners of *lascivious* lyricks ;" one of whom once enjoyed the hospitalities of this country, and evinced his gratitude by the defamation of Washington. Such " spawners of *lascivious* lyricks" as scatter imitations of Anacreon, Catullus and Ovid over the shelves of the young, to taint their lips with gilded impurity and to distil into their hearts the unholy essence of all that is mawkish in sentiment or infidel in belief. If such authors are thought by the reviewer to confer most " benefit on mankind ;" or even " the inventors of Congreve rockets and Shrapnel shells," or the pilferers of Grecian statuary—be it so : and let the rest of the world decide whether ours, in the language of this patriotic critic, be "the base Carthagenian greatness such as after times will never point to but by way of derision and warning."

Why is it another theme of complaint, that these remarks fell from the lips of Mr. Adams, and not of some obscure individual ? In a free government it can hardly be expected, that the tongue or the press will never sound discordant to the ears of monarchs. But this dandy reviewer may cherish "the sweet hope," that even our national anniversary will cease to be celebrated, because it brings unsavoury subjects between " the wind and his nobility." While the celebration continues, however, if our orators must talk of England, her kings and oppressions, or be silent concerning what produced Independence and what fills the Declaration which accompanied it; who are better qualified to discuss such themes than the first men of the republic? They did not hesitate at Athens, twice to appoint Pericles, to deliver public orations. The phillippics of Demosthenes, too, would probably be pronounced by the reviewer, like the address of Mr. Adams, inappropriate and " unnecessary." It would be easy also to call them mere " tirades" against the prince and country, that conspired to overthrow the liberties of Greece. Hancock and Warren, on the 5th of March, were called to address their fellow citizens in commemoration of British wrongs. And is their memory to be blackened by degenerate sycophants, because they obeyed the call, and applied to the English, who were attempting to enslave America, the epithets of " bloody butchers," " unfeeling ruffians"? The ashes of Patrick Henry, too, may be disturbed with another cry of "treason," because he declared that "Cæsar had his Brutus, Charles I. his Cromwell, and George III.---may profit by their example."

It is vain to hope, that this celebration or its principles will prove perpetual, unless our minds are recalled to the causes of it : and none are more competent to this duty than men like Mr. Adams, whose standing in society, whose eloquence and patriotism are calculated to shed over those causes the deathless light of truth. When Mr. Rush was a member of the cabinet, he delivered an oration on the same occasion, without giving rise to any strictures on its propriety. The Marquis of Londonderry, to be sure, might not condescend to comply with so plebeian a request as to address an audience of mere people ! But God forbid, that the men who fill our offices, should think themselves more than men ;—and should even a President of the United States disdain to consult the feelings of the people at large—disregard their opinions—separate from their interests, and assume a contemptuous hauteur towards his political creators,—he will soon see the hand upon the wall which writes his doom. But though this paragon of a Marquis might not submit to appear before such audiences as were addressed by Pericles, Hancock and Adams; yet the parliamentary debates of "the greatest nation on earth" are defiled with innumerable instances of vulgar abuse on America, from the titled mob both spiritual and temporal. Those periodical publications, too, which are the mirror of public taste, even as recently as the last numbers from England, have the effrontery to allege, that the Americans are "contemptible in open warfare, and void of discipline and courage to withstand the bayonet." This, it is to be remembered, falls from them after the experience of the battle of Bridgewater and the sortie from Fort Erie. They then add, to the indignation we trust of every civilized heart, not British, that the "brown Indian" is the only "suitable force to contend with them." Yes, "the brown Indian"—to tomahawk infants and females on our frontier, and, as at the River Raisin, to butcher prisoners, while unarmed, and confiding in British faith!

We have one recommendation to give to those young patricians in "the Emporium of Literature," who are pointing their Lilliputian needles at Mr. Adams. Let them be persuaded to peruse the orations there delivered to commemorate the British massacre of the 5th of March—let them meditate on the temper, style and sentiments of the public documents of our revolution—let the Declaration of Independence become a text book:—and then, if Mr. Adams and his address still continue subjects " of mortification," they must also blush at the mention of their fathers ; and the blood of those who declared it "immortality to die for one's country" in a war with England—will in vain cry to them from the ground " to scorn to be slaves."

The writer of these hasty remarks is no apologist of Mr. Adams. But he is the fearless advocate of truth, eloquence and patriotism. I have not the honour of even a personal acquaintance with him. But I am an AMERICAN, and I venerate the statesman, whose hands, " in these piping times" of sycophancy are pure from British predilections and British politics. I have neither smiles to ask nor adulation to bestow. The rising and the setting sun are alike to me.—But I am a REPUBLICAN---and from my soul do loathe the citizen of a republican government, who heaps abuse on its advocates, who sneers at our revolutionary principles, who invokes sympathy and admiration for those that starved our fathers in prison ships and murdered our mothers with the scalping knife of the "brown Indian." I rejoice no less than others at the prospect of "an era of good feelings." But I will never forget, under the penalty that my God may forget me, that these states are not now British provinces and that " a wall of partition," high as Heaven, exists between the foundations of our government and that of England ; and that the curse of a traitor should light on him, who attempts to cover this distinction from the people and to drag them into indifference concerning its importance.

It is true, that only the Hellespont rolled between free Greece and corrupting Asia ; while an Atlantick spreads between us and Europe. But the same pestilence, which crossed to the destruction of her republics in the luxuries of commerce, the contagion of manners and the enervating influence of some of the arts, may in the same modes, aided by the wings of the press, cross even a wider space to our perdition. Rome talked much of Cincinnatus. But in every county and in almost every village we have citizens, who serve the state, and are found at the plough. The humble occupations of our statesmen are themes of reproach with English travellers and journals. But we thank God, that so much of the patriarchal simplicity, frugality and industry of our ancestors yet lives. And the execrations of all good men ought to blast the wretch, who strives to assimilate us in either manners, morals or politics to one of the most corrupt monarchies in Christendom. We say one of the most corrupt ; and if our remark be questioned, we need appeal to no witnesses beyond ——— her present immaculate King and Queen ! But we would be guilty of neither injustice nor uncharitableness even to England. Her population yet retain some virtues. She has numerous proud recollections. Her character for bravery, enterprize and literary talent has covered her with imperishable glory : and long, very long has she averted, by the aid of these, the catastrophe, which awaits her insatiable spirit of aggrandizement, her financial embarrassments and her cruel oppressions in both hemispheres. What, too, if the sun never sets upon her territory ? What if a hundred millions of human beings yield obeisance to her flag ! Yet she was once our step-mother. Her King was our "tyrant."---She has since stretched her giant arm across the ocean again to crush us----she still wages an inveterate war against our "good name." And it is vain to hope, that legitimacy will ever cease to slander, and, if possible, put down the only surviving example of what she styles "successful rebellion."

We are aware, that the attacks on Mr. Adams's address may have been sharpened by causes which do not meet the ear. He has splendid qualifications to fill the highest office in the Union. If some Cataline or his incendiaries, in the strife, for supremacy, are already scattering firebrands and poison, it behoves every well wisher to the republic to awake. It is one of Mr. Adams's peculiar excellencies that while he is second to none in talents and experience, he makes neither personal influence nor exertion for what should always be the free gift of a free people. The discussion is premature. The election and its various bearings too distant. But in the mean time, if the character of Mr. Adams is destined to be mangled and even crucified to gratify British sycophants or the sinister views of demagogues, whose path to office is obstructed by his virtues; let the tempest rage—

_____ " An honest man is still an unmoved rock,
　　　　Washed whiter, but not shaken by the shock."

CPSIA information can be obtained
at www.ICGtesting.com
Printed in the USA
BVHW071414090119
537429BV00013B/1349/P